PAINTERS OF THE
CAVES

BY PATRICIA LAUBER

HAMPTON-BROWN

THE EXCHANGE

Why do people create and enjoy art?

The author gratefully acknowledges the comments of expert
Dr. Ian Tattersall, Curator and Chairman, Department of Anthropology,
American Museum of Natural History.

The cave painting on the front cover is from Lascaux. It shows a foal and
an aurochs. The back cover painting, from Chauvet, shows a rhinoceros. The
title page shows the hand of a Stone Age person stenciled on a cave wall.

Reprinted with permission of the National Geographic Society
from the book *Painters of the Caves* by Patricia Lauber.
Text copyright © 1998 Patricia Lauber.

On-Page Coach ™ (introductions, questions, on-page glossaries),
The Exchange, back cover summary © Hampton-Brown.

Hampton-Brown
P.O. Box 223220
Carmel, California 93922
800-333-3510
www.hampton-brown.com

Printed in the United States of America

ISBN-13: 978-0-7362-2807-7
ISBN-10: 0-7362-2807-1

06 07 08 09 10 11 12 13 14 10 9 8 7 6 5 4 3 2

Contents

1. A Great Discovery   **5**

2. People of the Ice Age   **11**

3. A New Way of Life   **17**

4. Stone Age Artists   **23**

5. What the Art May Tell   **31**

6. The Importance of Chauvet   **39**

Appendix 45

Selected Bibliography 46

Index 47

Explorers discover a cave. The walls of the cave are covered with more than 300 paintings. The paintings are 32,000 years old.

A Great Discovery

One chilly afternoon in December 1994, three old friends met to go exploring. The three—two men and a woman—**shared a great enthusiasm**: searching for caves in the limestone hills near Avignon, in southeast France.

Limestone is fairly soft rock. Long ago, over many years, the Ardèche River carved deep gorges in these hills, creating cliffs of limestone. The cliffs are **honeycombed with** caves, some hollowed out by underground rivers, some by rainwater that sank in and dissolved the limestone.

For thousands of years, starting in the Stone Age, people used these caves and left behind **traces** of themselves. In their exploring, the three friends had found several caves with traces of wall art done by Stone Age painters. They hoped to find more, but what they found that December day was something they had only dreamed about.

They followed an ancient mule path up a cliff and arrived at a narrow ledge. An opening in the cliff led to a pile of rocks where they could feel air coming out—the sign of a cave. Tearing away the rocks, they uncovered a small passageway, just big enough for a person to wriggle through.

Exploring caves is dangerous. It is all too easy to get stuck, to take a bad fall, to become lost. But the three had twenty years of experience and they had come equipped with lights, ropes, and a ladder. **They pressed ahead.**

....

shared a great enthusiasm had the same favorite activity
honeycombed with full of
traces evidence
They pressed ahead. They went into the cave.

(Left) Caves riddle the limestone cliffs of gorges carved long ago by the Ardèche River.

One of the three explorers, Jean-Marie Chauvet, examines a panel of horse heads in the cave that was named for him in southeastern France. Chauvet is a source of much new information about the painters of the caves.

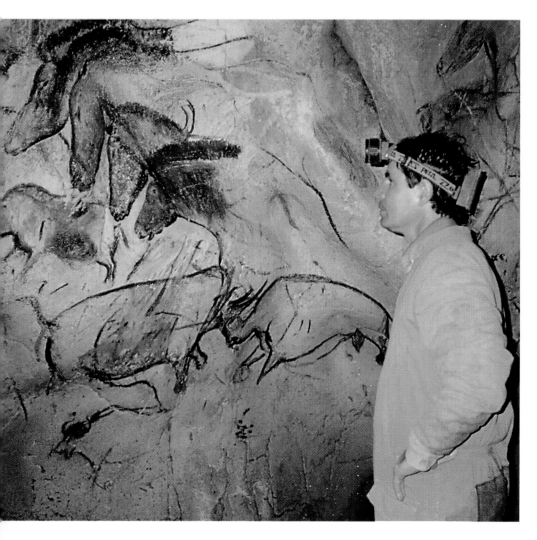

The woman went first, lying on her stomach. At the end of the passageway was a 30-foot drop to the cave floor. Their ladder took them down. The cave was so big that darkness swallowed their lights; they could hardly see the walls. Moving with care, they came to a place where the floor of the cave was **strewn** with bear bones and teeth, where bears had dug **hollows to hibernate in**.

Moments later they saw a drawing of a little red mammoth on a spur of rock. As they looked around, a 3-foot-high bear loomed before them on a white wall. Discovery followed discovery—a huge red rhinoceros, a big mammoth, a bear or lion, human handprints stenciled on the walls.

They had made a truly great discovery. The cave, named Chauvet after one of the explorers, holds more than 300 paintings of animals that lived some 32,000 years ago, late in the Stone Age: horses, bears, hyenas, woolly rhinos, mammoths, bison, wild cattle, lions, deer, panthers, mountain goats. Drawn in black, red, and yellow, they **parade** across rock walls, sometimes leaping or running.

....

strewn covered

hollows to hibernate in holes to sleep in during the winter months

parade look as if they are moving

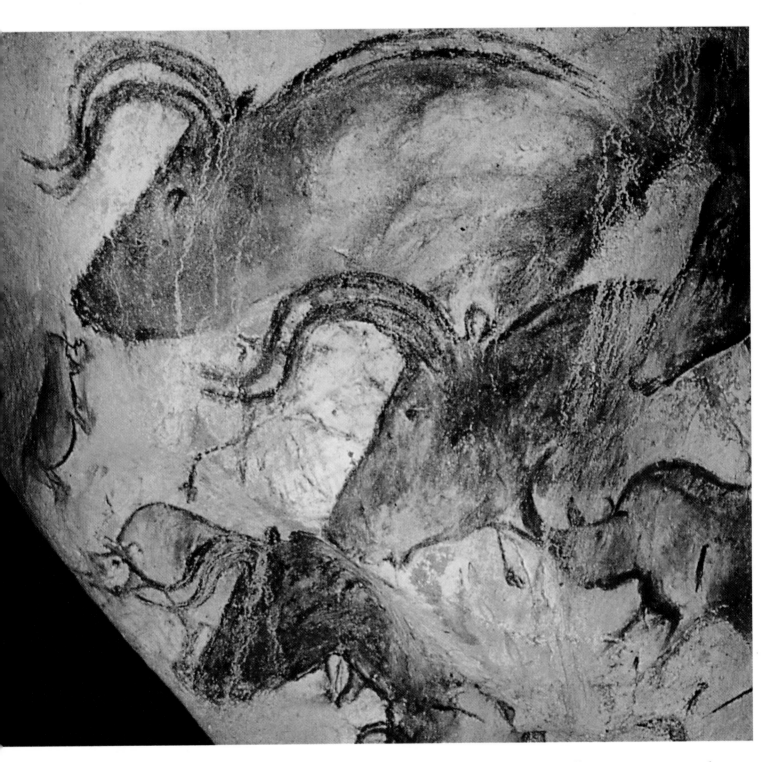

To the left of the panel of horse heads, cave artists painted aurochs (ancestors of today's cattle) and rhinoceroses.

Chauvet is **far from** the only cave with Stone Age wall paintings. Most such caves **lie to** the west, in southwest France and northern Spain. Some are found elsewhere in Europe and on other continents from Africa to Australia. But Chauvet is one of the biggest and best, and it is the oldest known. Because its original entrance had been blocked by a rockfall, no one else had visited the cave for thousands of years.

....

far from not
lie to are in

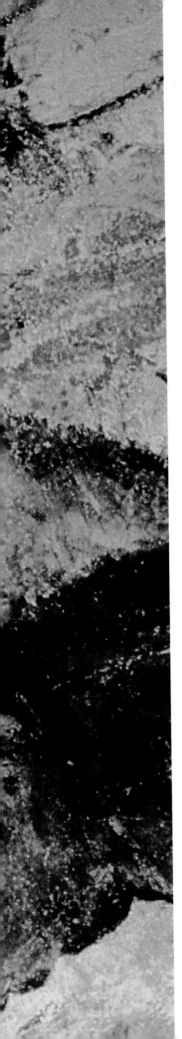

Ice Age horses were short and stocky, about the size of today's ponies. The animal at lower left is a rhinoceros.

The names of the cave artists are long lost. They could not sign their names, because they lived before writing was invented. But we do know something about them. They were people like us, modern human beings.

Their story has been **pieced together** by scientists who study **ancient peoples**. Part of the story is told by fossils, which are traces of ancient life. A fossil can be many things. The footprints of Stone Age artists who worked in the caves are fossils, as are the footprints of children who played there. But most fossils are skulls, bones, and teeth—hard parts of the body that were **preserved** when rock formed around them. Another part of the story is told by stone tools and other objects that people left behind and that, in time, became buried under dust, dirt, and rock.

The first modern humans to live in Europe are sometimes called Cro-Magnons, for the rock-shelter in France where their fossils and stone tools were first found. More often today, they are called early modern humans. They arrived in the Middle East and Europe during the Ice Age.

....

pieced together figured out

ancient peoples people who lived long ago

preserved saved

BEFORE YOU MOVE ON...

1. **Main Idea and Details** List details that support this main idea: The Chauvet cave paintings were a very important discovery.

2. **Cause and Effect** Reread page 9. Why don't we know the names of the cave artists?

LOOK AHEAD Read pages 10–15 to learn how early modern humans changed.

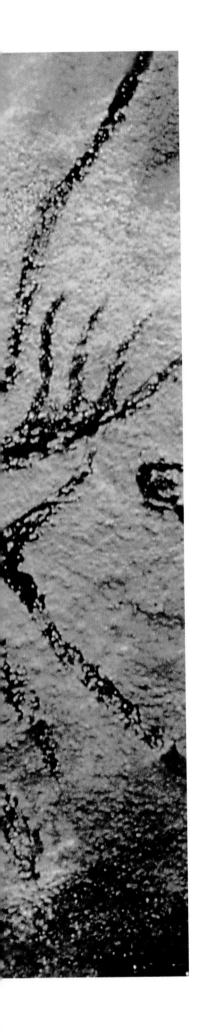

During the Ice Age, early modern humans begin to leave Africa. They invent new tools and find new ways of making them.

2

People of the Ice Age

There are times when, in the far places of the earth, more snow falls in winter than the summer sun can melt. In these places—polar lands and lofty mountains—the snow builds up over thousands of years. Under the weight of new snow, the old packs down into ice. Finally, under great weight, the ice begins to **flow**.

Mountain glaciers reach down into valleys. Sheets of ice spread over the land. Once-green lands are swallowed by ice a mile or more thick. Winds blowing over the ice reach far away. Winters are long and cold. Summers are short and cool.

These times are known as ice ages. Each time, ice **advanced over** the land for thousands of years before the climate warmed. Then the towering sheets of ice melted and shrank, releasing floods of water. In the warming climate, life came back to land left bare by ice. Then, once more, the ice began to build. The last period of great growth began about 115,000 years ago and ended 10,000 years ago. It is known as the Ice Age.

During the Ice Age there were many swings of climate, times when temperatures rose, melting ice for a few hundred years, until the cold returned.

With each change in climate, plant life changed. As the ice advanced, forests **gave way to** grasslands, then grasslands became tundra, frozen land where only sedges, mosses, and lichens grew. When the ice shrank and land thawed, grasslands spread and then forests **took root**.

As plant life moved north or south, animals moved in search of food. People followed the animals.

....

flow move across the land
advanced over came and covered
gave way to turned into
took root grew

(Left) Reindeer were a major source of food for Ice Age peoples. These deer, from the Lascaux cave, appear to be swimming a river.

A computer program produced this image of what a young Neanderthal may have looked like. The early modern humans of Europe looked like Europeans of today.

It was during the Ice Age, probably about 100,000 years ago, that modern humans began to spread out of Africa, where they had first appeared. **They went on, most scientists think, to inhabit the world**, becoming the ancestors of us all. One group stayed in the Middle East, where they **overlapped with** an earlier people. These earlier people were the Neanderthals, who are named for the Neander Valley in Germany, where their fossils were first discovered.

....

They went on, most scientists think, to inhabit the world
Most scientists think that the modern humans lived all over the world

overlapped with lived at the same time as

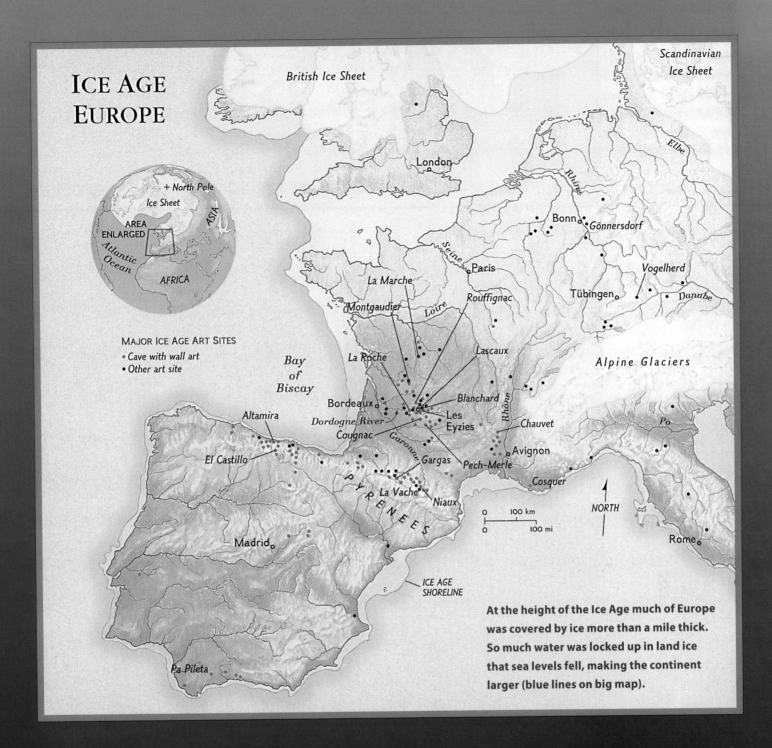

ICE AGE EUROPE

Scandinavian Ice Sheet

British Ice Sheet

+ North Pole
Ice Sheet

AREA ENLARGED

ASIA

Atlantic Ocean

AFRICA

London

Elbe

Rhine

Bonn
Gönnersdorf

Seine
Paris

Vogelherd

Tübingen

Danube

La Marche

Rouffignac

Montgaudier

Loire

MAJOR ICE AGE ART SITES
• Cave with wall art
• Other art site

La Roche

Lascaux

Alpine Glaciers

Bay of Biscay

Altamira

Bordeaux

Blanchard

Les Eyzies

Rhône

Po

Dordogne River

Chauvet

El Castillo

Cougnac

Garonne

Avignon

Gargas

Pech-Merle

PYRENEES

La Vache

Cosquer

Niaux

0   100 km
0   100 mi

NORTH

Madrid

Rome

Pa Pileta

ICE AGE SHORELINE

At the height of the Ice Age much of Europe
was covered by ice more than a mile thick.
So much water was locked up in land ice
that sea levels fell, making the continent
larger (blue lines on big map).

Arriving in Europe during the Ice Age, early modern humans usually settled along rivers. Places where their artwork has been found are shown on the map.

The two groups looked very different. Neanderthals were short and **stocky**, with **barrel** chests, big bones, and strong muscles. A Neanderthal face had a ridge of bone across the brow; both the forehead and the chin sloped backward.

The early moderns **were built** like us. They were taller and slimmer, with smaller faces and steep foreheads. Their jaws were short and had chins.

....

stocky wide
barrel rounded
were built looked

13

At one time, Neanderthals and early moderns made the same kinds of tools, such as the double-edged scraper, which is 3½ inches long. They struck flakes from flint cores. The core shown is 4 inches wide.

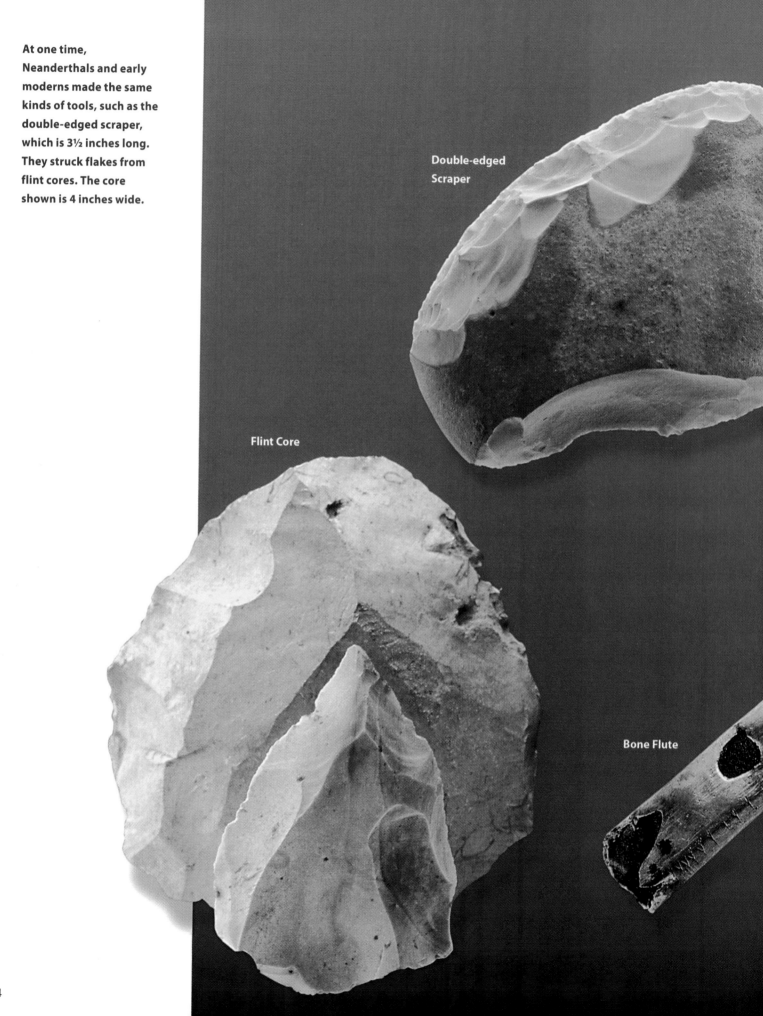

Double-edged Scraper

Flint Core

Bone Flute

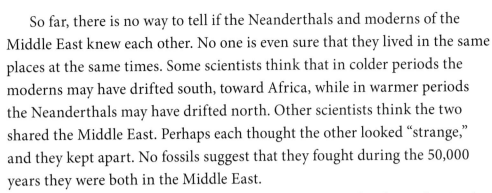

Bird-bone flutes date back at least 32,000 years. The whole flute was, of course, longer than this 3½-inch-long fragment.

So far, there is no way to tell if the Neanderthals and moderns of the Middle East knew each other. No one is even sure that they lived in the same places at the same times. Some scientists think that in colder periods the moderns may have drifted south, toward Africa, while in warmer periods the Neanderthals may have drifted north. Other scientists think the two shared the Middle East. Perhaps each thought the other looked "strange," and they kept apart. No fossils suggest that they fought during the 50,000 years they were both in the Middle East.

For much of the time, the two lived the same way. They hunted animals and gathered plant foods. They made the same sorts of stone tools, which served as knives, scrapers, axes, and perhaps spear points. They used fire to warm themselves and for cooking.

For a long time, they seem to have been **evenly matched**, with equal skills and tools. And then a big change took place in the modern humans. It was as if an unused part of their brains had suddenly **come awake**. They became fully modern, in mind as well as body.

We may never know how or why this big change took place. But stone tools tell part of what happened. The modern humans **became prolific inventors**. They invented new tools and new ways of making them. Perhaps with these advances the moderns were able to move into Europe, where Neanderthals had been living for some 150,000 years. Or perhaps the advances were made after they reached Europe. But by 40,000 years ago the moderns were spread from Bulgaria to Spain.

In the years ahead, they would discover new and better ways of hunting.

They would become painters, carvers, engravers, in a great burst of creative energy. They would make and play musical instruments made of animal bones—flutes, rattles, drums.

And in the years ahead, another big change would also take place. The Neanderthals would disappear. Their way of life had served them well for a long time. But it seems they were no match for the modern humans and their new ways of life.

....

evenly matched very similar

come awake started to work

became prolific inventors created many new things

BEFORE YOU MOVE ON...

1. **Conclusions** Reread page 15. Early modern humans became inventors. How did this help them?

2. **Viewing** Look at the map on page 13. How does it help you understand the Ice Age better?

LOOK AHEAD Read pages 16–21 to learn about the modern humans' new way of life.

With the help of their spear-throwers, these hunters hope to bring down an ibex, or wild goat (top), and a migrating reindeer. Both drawings were made by an artist of today.

Antler Harpoon Head

Willow Leaf Point

3

A New Way of Life

Neanderthals kept making the same tools and weapons. The moderns kept inventing new and better kinds. They were **choosy** about the kinds of stones they used. They learned to get many flakes from one core of stone, instead of one or two. They thought of new tools and made what they needed, working **from a design that was only in their heads**. They made long, slender blades, scrapers with a curved surface, fine-pointed tools for piercing and engraving, tiny stone tools that were fitted to handles. They carved and polished bone, antler, and ivory to make still other tools.

They became better hunters. They invented a spear-thrower, which helped them throw a spear farther. They invented a barbed tip for harpoons, which stuck in the flesh of fish and small animals. By late in the Ice Age, some 14,000 years ago, they had invented the bow and arrow.

While the Neanderthals spent much time looking for food, the moderns learned that animals move with the seasons. At one time of year salmon swam up rivers to **spawn**.

....

choosy careful
from a design that was only in their heads without written plans
spawn lay eggs

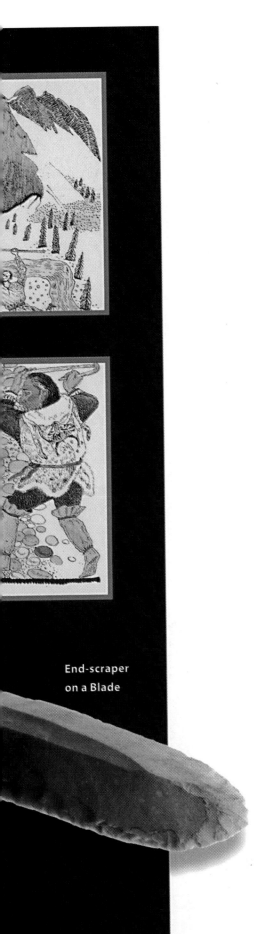

End-scraper on a Blade

(Left) Early moderns invented many new tools. They may also have invented a calendar. At least one scientist thinks the markings on this piece of bone (above) show the changing moon that marked the passing seasons.

An artist of today shows a rock-shelter (left) where thousands of fish bones have been found. Probably groups of Stone Age people met here at times when the salmon were running. They may have sun-dried fish as a winter's food supply.

Stacked mammoth jaws surround this Stone Age house (above) in Ukraine, as drawn by the same artist.

At another time, migrating reindeer had to cross a certain river and were easy to spear. The moderns camped at places where food would be plentiful, going there at the right time of year. Probably they had discovered **how to keep track of the seasons**.

They also learned to preserve food. Fish, for example, were dried in the sun or smoked over fires. To the north, in Ukraine, moderns dug pits in the frozen soil of the **tundra**. The pits became freezers, where mammoth and reindeer meat could be stored.

Ukraine was a good hunting ground, with big herds of large mammals. But its climate was one of the harshest on earth. This was a land of bitter cold, near the advancing sheets of ice. To the south, moderns often took shelter, as Neanderthals did, in the entrances to caves or under **rock overhangs**. In Ukraine, there were no caves. The moderns made shelters from what they had—animal skins and mammoth bones. They had the bones of mammoths they had killed, and they had the bones of mammoths that had died naturally over many years.

One bone house was made of nearly 400 mammoth bones, a weight of 23 tons. Layers of skull, shoulder, and other bones formed an inside wall. It was strengthened by an outer wall made of 95 jawbones stacked chin down. The roof was made of skins and arching tusks, forming a shelter that measured 13½ feet across. At one camp there were at least 5 of these houses.

....

how to keep track of the seasons how to figure out when the seasons would change

tundra cold ground

rock overhangs places where a rock sheltered the ground

Trees grow poorly in the frozen ground of Ukraine. Lacking wood, the moderns used mammoth bones to feed the fires that heated their shelters.

In both northern and southern Europe, Stone Age peoples must have worn clothing to keep warm. Even in the sheltered valleys of southwestern France, the climate was cool.

The Neanderthals may have wrapped themselves in animal skins held in place by strips of hide. Probably the moderns did the same at first. But then they invented tools that could be used **as punches**. They may have laced skins together. And by 26,000 years ago they had invented bone needles. Sewing became possible. About the same time, they invented buttons, made from stone or bone; whether the buttons served as fasteners or only as decorations, no one knows.

Both the Neanderthals and modern humans used fire for cooking and for warming themselves. Neanderthal **hearths** were either flat or hollowed out. Moderns discovered how to make better hearths with hotter fires. They dug pits and lined these with stones, which both held and gave off heat. They surrounded the hearths with flat stones, which could be used in cooking. They realized that fires burned better when given more air and **dug channels to create a draft**.

The moderns also found new uses for fire. They heated stones and used them to heat water in skin-lined pits. By 26,000 years ago, modern humans had invented kilns, ovens in which small clay figures were fired. They also invented lamps that gave off light when animal fat was burned through wicks of juniper twigs.

Fires, warm clothing, and mammoth bone shelters let modern humans live in the harsh climate to the north, where the big game roamed and the hunting was good.

....

as punches to make small holes in the animal skins

hearths fireplaces

dug channels to create a draft dug holes around the fire to get more air

In both north and south, fires and hearths brought people together at day's end. Around a fire, they shared food and thoughts, for no one doubts that the modern humans could talk—scientists are not sure about the Neanderthals. If the moderns made furniture of wood, it has, like their clothing, **rotted away**. But fossil pollen shows that they did bring armloads of grasses into their shelters, to serve as beds.

The shelters and campsites of the moderns vary in size. There are places where small **bands lived, perhaps ranging widely in search of game**. There are other places where bands came together when food was plentiful. Perhaps these were times for finding mates from other bands. Perhaps, too, trade took place or there was an exchange of gifts, for amber from the north has turned up at campsites in southern Europe and seashells from the Mediterranean in the north.

About 5,000 years after modern humans brought a new way of life to Europe, Neanderthals disappear from the fossil record. No evidence shows the moderns **set upon** the Neanderthals and killed them. The best guess is that faced with fully modern humans, the Neanderthals retreated into places where there were no moderns. There they lived in small bands, apart from other Neanderthals. Without a chance to meet other groups and find mates, the Neanderthals died out.

With their new way of life, modern humans were highly successful. They lived well, and they did not have to spend all their time looking for food. They had leisure. Perhaps some used that time for art. Or perhaps each group supplied its artists with food. In either case, they were people who created and liked art.

....

rotted away been destroyed

bands lived, perhaps ranging widely in search of game groups of people lived, perhaps moving a lot to search for animals to eat

set upon attacked

The moderns cooked liquid foods, such as broths and porridge, in pits of hot stones that were probably lined with skins. The drawing is by an artist of today.

BEFORE YOU MOVE ON...

1. **Main Idea and Details** Find details to support this main idea: With their new way of life, modern humans were highly successful.

2. **Comparisons** How were the fires made by the Neanderthals and modern humans different? How were they the same?

LOOK AHEAD Read pages 22–29. What materials did the modern humans use to make their paintings?

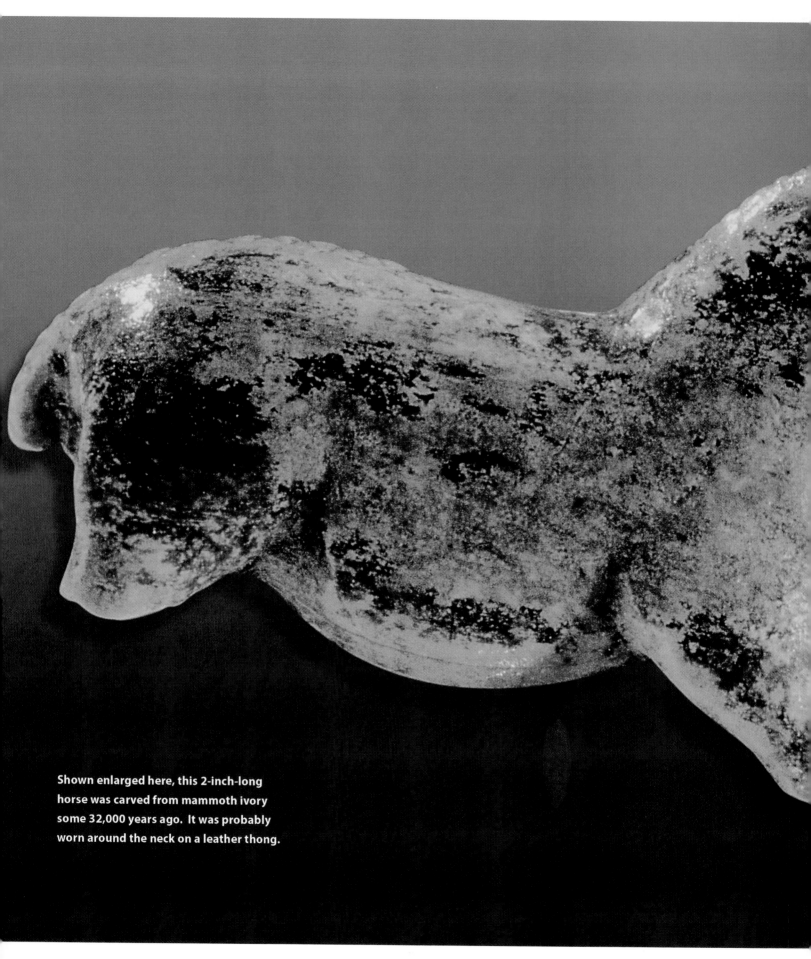

Shown enlarged here, this 2-inch-long
horse was carved from mammoth ivory
some 32,000 years ago. It was probably
worn around the neck on a leather thong.

Artists of the Stone Age created a lot of art. Most of their art shows animals that were important in their lives.

Stone Age Artists

No one knows when modern humans first became artists. Good art seems to appear suddenly. If there were earlier **works**, they have not been found—or have not survived. But the artists used their talents in many ways and made use of many materials.

They made small objects that could be worn or carried around. They pierced and strung seashells and animal teeth to wear as necklaces, earrings, bracelets. They carved animal figures out of mammoth ivory and also used ivory to make beads that decorated clothing. Three bodies found in a grave in Russia each had 3,500 beads of mammoth ivory, arranged in rows. The clothing had rotted away, but the rows suggest that the beads were strung and the strings sewn to the clothing. One scientist found by experimenting that it takes 45 minutes to make a bead. And so each body had 2,625 hours of beadwork buried with it. The people in the grave must have been important.

....

works pieces of art

Realistic human figures and faces are seldom found in Stone Age art. This 5-inch-high ivory head is a rare example.

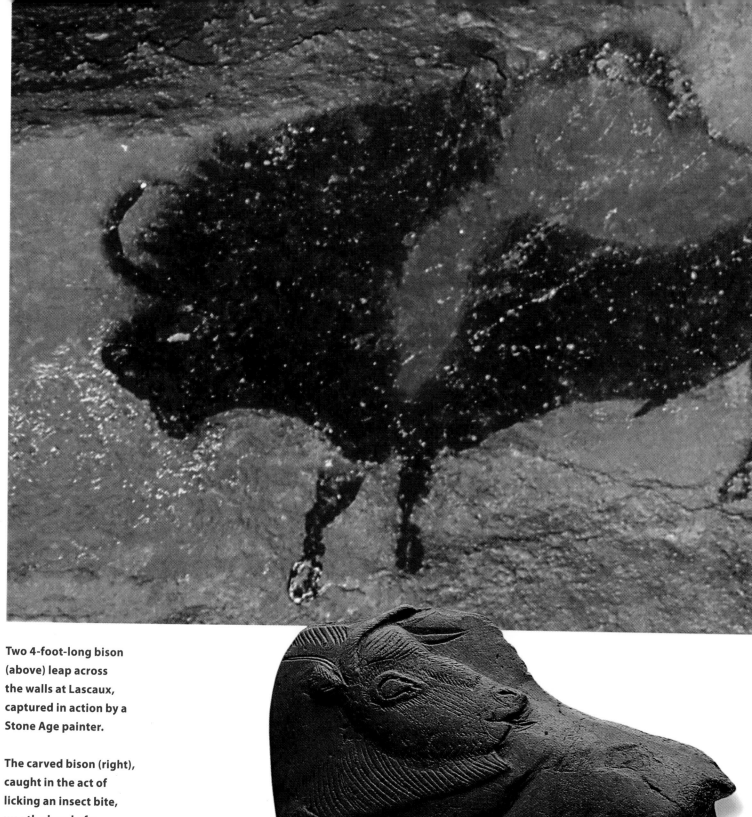

Two 4-foot-long bison (above) leap across the walls at Lascaux, captured in action by a Stone Age painter.

The carved bison (right), caught in the act of licking an insect bite, was the head of a spear-thrower and is about 3½ inches long.

The carved bear's head (far right) is about 1½ inches long.

Using sharp tools, artists **engraved** bones, antlers, pebbles, and slabs of stone that were used to pave cave floors. The art often showed animals. In time, artists began to engrave weapons and everyday tools as well as art objects. They made small clay figures of animals and women and hardened them in kilns.

When bands of people came together at big campsites, did they exchange art? Was some jewelry a **badge of** membership in a certain group? Were some pieces lucky charms? There is no way to tell.

The artists who worked in caves often engraved the walls. Some of the engravings are done **in fine line** and are almost invisible when lighted from

....

engraved carved into
badge of sign of; way to show
in fine line using thin lines

Scientists think the moderns may have stenciled their handprints on walls by blowing paint through a tube, as shown in this recent drawing.

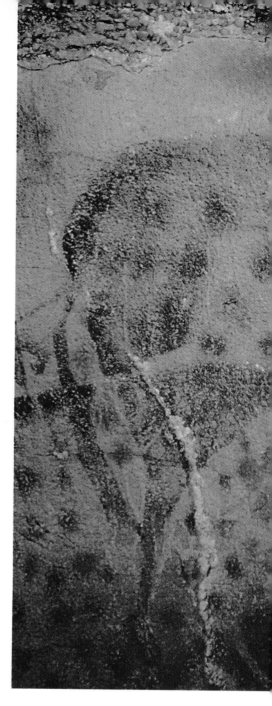

the front. They seem to leap out when lighted from the side. Perhaps lighting was used for magic—making animals appear and disappear.

Some of the cave artists **worked in clay**—engraving the cave floor or sculpting **banks** of clay.

And some artists drew or painted on the cave walls. Their colors were red, yellow, brown, and black. At times they used charcoal for black, but mostly they took their colors from **minerals that could be ground** into powder or turned into a

....

worked in clay used clay to make art

banks piles

minerals that could be ground materials from the earth that they crushed

The human handprints give an idea of scale in the painting of this Stone Age horse filled with dots at Pech-Merle.

kind of crayon. The powder had to be mixed with something to make paint. To find out what **that something was**, one scientist **carried out** 205 experiments with cave painting over three years. In the end, he discovered that what worked best was water, especially cave water.

To apply the paint, artists sometimes used their fingers. Sometimes they used a pad of animal fur. But usually they painted with brushes made from animal hair or crushed twigs.

Handprints are common in caves. Some were created by a palm coated with paint. Most were stenciled by blowing paint from a tube or perhaps from the mouth.

....

that something was the artists mixed the powder with
carried out did

27

An artist of today imagines a Stone Age artist standing on a scaffold and painting an aurochs. Light in the caves came from torches and from fat-burning limestone lamps like this one, which is about 8 inches long.

Artists painted on ceilings and high walls as well as surfaces they could reach easily. To get up, they must have used ladders, probably tree trunks with stubs of branches. In at least one cave—Lascaux—they built a **scaffold**.

The depths of caves are dark. To see, the artists needed light. It came from torches of wood and from lamps that burned animal fat. A few deep caves also have hearths, where fires may have given off a strong light.

There were also places where artists worked outdoors, engraving, and probably painting, on rock-faces. A few of these engravings have been found in sheltered places. Many others must have weathered away. Outdoor art may have been the way a group **staked its claim to** a certain region.

The world of the modern humans was the world of nature. In it they found food, clothing, and shelter. They observed it closely, so closely that artists working in caves, without models, were able to draw from memory.

The animals they painted most often were horses and bison—the forest-dwelling bison of Europe, which are different from the bison of the American plains. Caves also **hold** many pictures of wild cattle, deer, goats, and mammoths. Bears and lions appear. Many animals are rare—the rhinoceros, musk-ox, ass, wolf, fox, hyena. There are few fish, birds, or reptiles. Plants are also rare, although they were important foods.

Few human figures appear in cave art, but a number of figures appear to be part human, part animal—or perhaps humans wearing animal masks and skins.

Like the art that could be carried around, cave art also includes markings that are not pictures. There are many, many dots. There are circles, rectangles, zigzags, grids, and other signs, as well as stencils and prints of hands.

No one today knows what the signs mean. No one knows what the paintings mean. But scientists and others who study the art have some ideas.

scaffold tall platform
staked its claim to showed that they owned
hold have

BEFORE YOU MOVE ON...

1. **Main Idea and Details** List details to support this main idea: Artists used materials from nature to make cave paintings.

2. **Categorizing** What kinds of art objects did the modern humans make?

LOOK AHEAD Read pages 30–37 to learn theories about why the art was made.

Scientists have different ideas about what the art means. We may never know the truth, but there are good theories.

5

What the Art May Tell

Cave paintings were not a way of decorating shelters, for people seldom lived deep within caves. Nor were the paintings done for fun. Dark, damp, and slippery, the caves were not pleasant places to work. Some pictures were painted in **nooks and crannies** that were hard to squeeze into. Ceilings and other high places required ladders or scaffolds. Art must have **played an important part in** the lives of modern humans and had meaning for them.

What did it mean?

Because the art shows mostly animals, some people have thought that the paintings were hunting magic. There may be some truth in that idea, but it cannot be the whole story. It does not, for example, explain why there are so few reindeer and birds, both of which were important foods. One cave has more horses than any other animal; yet bones at the nearby campsite show that the people ate mostly reindeer. At another cave, the paintings show horses and mammoths; again, bones tell of reindeer. Also, hunting magic does not explain rhinos and lions, which were not food.

Another idea has to do with beliefs. The moderns almost certainly believed in powerful spirits. Actions of these spirits would explain many mysterious things: thunder and lightning, the coming of spring, good or poor hunting, the rising and setting of the sun.

....

nooks and crannies small areas
played an important part in been an important part of

(Left) Stone Age artists often worked cave features into their paintings. Here, while painting an aurochs bull on a ceiling at Lascaux, an artist made a bulge in the rock part of the bull's shoulder. The artist also used the margin between light and dark limestone as the ground on which a line of horses, in winter coat, are walking.

A cave lion was engraved on rock at Trois-Frères cave. It is pitted, as if it had been struck by a blunt instrument. An artist of today imagines a shaman in antlered headdress (left) attacking the lion, perhaps as an aid in killing it.

At Chauvet (top), two mammoths were engraved, walking behind a horse.

There are tribes today with such beliefs. They have an important member called a shaman. A shaman is a person with spiritual powers who serves as healer, priest, and, most important, a link between this world and the spirit world. Shamans reach the spirit world when they are in a **trance**, and they see spirits in animal form.

Perhaps the cave animals **stand for** spirits being asked for help. Perhaps the spirits represented by horses and bison were the ones shamans most often appealed to.

Some scientists think that shamans may have done some of the paintings while in a trance. They think, too, that shamans are shown in cave art—they are the figures that seem to be part animal, part human, or a human wearing an animal mask and skin.

A third idea is that the painted caves were places where ceremonies were held, where young people were accepted as adults.

Still a fourth idea is that the cave paintings were aids to memory. People who cannot read and write—who cannot look something up in a book—must depend on memory. The history of the group, its beliefs and myths, its rules, its hunting methods and places—everything is stored in memory. To keep memories alive, people must pass them down.

trance condition like sleep
stand for represent

These Ice Age horses at Lascaux are thought to be related to some modern wild horses of Mongolia. They are known as Chinese Horses because they look like later Asian paintings. The barb in the aurochs, center, may be a spear. The paintings and engravings at Lascaux were done some 17,000 years ago.

Cave paintings may tell a story or remind the viewer of a story. Perhaps this is how young people learned about their history. Imagine you are led into a cave. Darkness swallows you. Every sense in your body is alert. The shaman starts to speak. Suddenly there is light. Adults have arrived with torches. In the flickering light, animals on the walls seem to move. **You are sent on** alone in the dark, crawling through narrow passageways, wading through water, stumbling over blocks of stone. Suddenly you **round** a corner and a moving bear appears on a wall, lighted by a lamp on the cave floor. The Shaman's voice follows you, telling of the time when....

....

You are sent on The adults tell you to walk

round turn

34

What you hear will make an impression on you. And each time you look at a painting, you will hear the shaman's voice again.

Today's scientists think there is probably some truth in all of these ideas. But we may never know the whole truth. Cave paintings and signs hold messages that were not addressed to us, and the time of great cave paintings came to an end before people had learned to record their beliefs in writing.

Life changed at the end of the Ice Age when a warm period began, the one in which we still live. The mile-high sheets of ice and the mountain glaciers melted and shrank. Over the next few thousand years, some animals, such as the mammoths, died out.

....

What you hear will make an impression on you. You will remember what you hear.

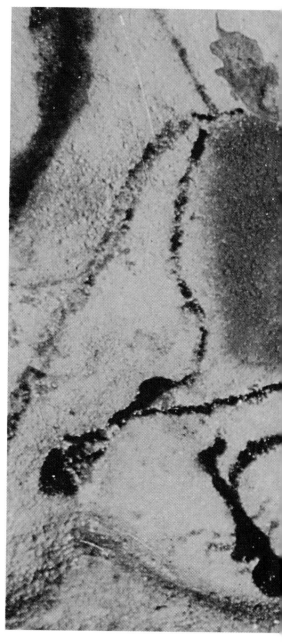

No one knows what the signs in the caves mean, but they must have had meaning to the people who made them and saw them.

Trees and forests came back and spread north. **Animals moved with the plants.**

Daily life became harder than it had been during the Ice Age. Hunting large game on open grasslands had been much easier than hunting deer and boars in the woods. Ways of life changed. Around this time another group of modern humans to the south and east **took a different kind of big step forward.** They discovered how to raise crops and herd animals. With this discovery people could **settle** in one place. First towns and then cities grew. People discovered metal. They invented writing.

....

Animals moved with the plants. Animals went to places where plants were growing.

took a different kind of big step forward changed their lives in a different way

settle live for a long time

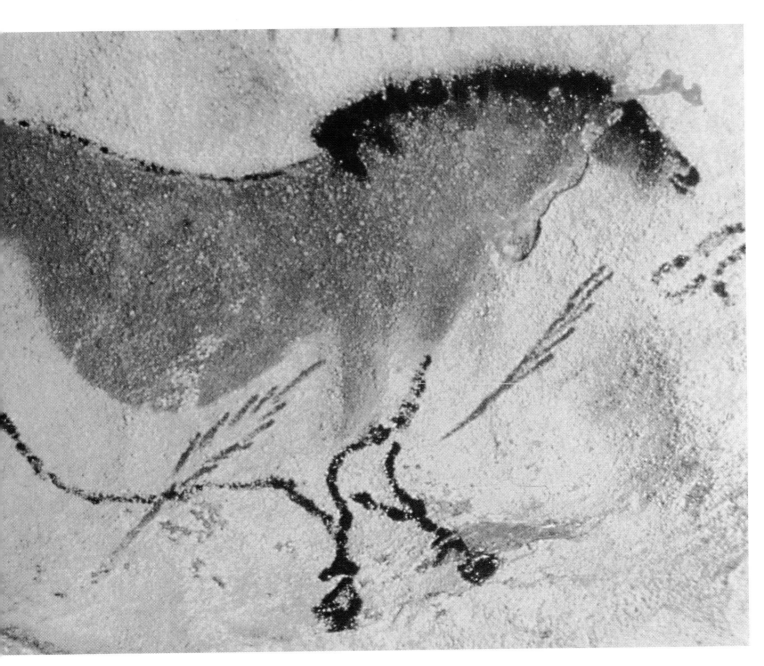

For many years, people thought this Lascaux painting showed a horse and harpoons. A newer idea is that it shows a horse and plants, which were an important food source.

The art of the Stone Age was forgotten, lying hidden in caves, where rockfalls often blocked the entrances. It was only in the 1870s that the world began to learn that great artists had worked in Europe thousands of years ago.

Much has been learned since then, and much remains to be discovered. That is one reason why the Chauvet cave is important.

BEFORE YOU MOVE ON...

1. **Viewing** Some scientists think the modern humans believed their art gave them power. Look at pages 32–33. How do the picture and caption help you understand this theory?

2. **Paraphrase** Reread page 33. In your own words, tell what this means: "To keep memories alive, people must pass them down."

LOOK AHEAD Read pages 38–43 to learn more about why the Chauvet paintings are important.

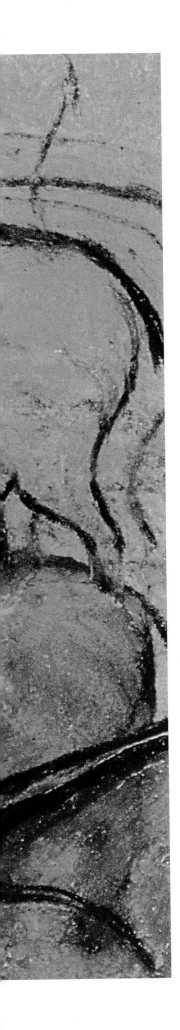

6

The Importance of Chauvet

At one time it seemed that all the great cave paintings had been done toward the end of the Ice Age, 17,000 to 14,000 years ago. Older paintings were **minor works**. Perhaps, some people said, the artists learned by **trial and error as they went along**. The discovery of the Chauvet cave proves that idea wrong. It shows that the first modern humans who reached Europe were talented artists. The Ice Age had more than one period of great art.

Chauvet is also important for its animals. The animal most often shown is the woolly rhino, not the horse or the bison. And there are many meat-eaters, such as lions and panthers. As one scientist said, the artists "had reindeer in their stomachs, but they had rhinos on their minds. They were painting animals that were good to think, not animals that were good to eat."

Chauvet is important, too, because it has been carefully guarded ever since its discovery. The three friends who found it knew that many caves have been damaged by visitors.

One of the most famous caves in France, Lascaux, was discovered in 1940, at the start of World War II. After the war thousands of visitors **flocked** to see it. Their feet packed down the cave floor, destroying evidence of the artists. Body heat and electric lights changed the temperature of the cave. Visitors breathed in the air, removing oxygen, and breathed out carbon

....

minor works not as good

trial and error as they went along trying different ways of painting before they found the best way

flocked came in crowds

(Left) An artist at Chauvet painted a herd of rhinoceroses.

39

Among the animals painted on the walls of Chauvet are bison (above), cave lions (top, right), and two rhinos facing each other.

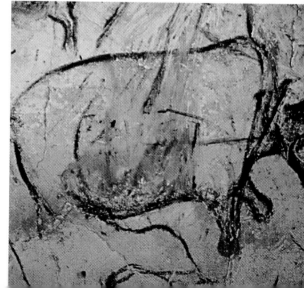

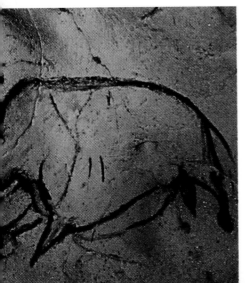

dioxide and water vapor, changing the atmosphere of the cave. Water vapor **condensed** on the walls and paintings. Molds began to grow on them. Seeing the damage, the French government closed the cave to visitors.

Chauvet is being preserved as it was found. In the years ahead, small groups of scientists will study it, finding it as it was left by the people **who were us**.

....

condensed gathered on
who were us who were humans, too

Chauvet, today.

BEFORE YOU MOVE ON...

1. **Conclusions** Reread page 39. Why are the animal paintings in Chauvet cave so important?

2. **Cause and Effect** What happened when visitors came to Lascaux cave? How did this affect Chauvet cave?

Appendix

Dating Ancient Life

Scientists who study the distant past date their finds in several ways, often using built-in atomic clocks. One of these clocks is called carbon 14. It is found in living and once-living things.

Carbon 14 forms in the atmosphere when atoms of carbon are bombarded by cosmic rays from space. Carbon-14 atoms are radioactive—that is, they keep breaking down and giving off tiny parts of themselves. When carbon 14 combines with oxygen, it forms radioactive carbon dioxide, which mixes with other carbon dioxide in the air.

Plants take in carbon dioxide to make their food, and so each plant contains a tiny amount of carbon 14. Animals eat plants or eat other animals that eat plants. Every animal's body contains a tiny amount of carbon 14. The carbon 14 in plants and animals keeps breaking down, but more of it keeps being added.

When an animal or plant dies, it stops taking in carbon 14. The carbon 14 already in its tissues goes on breaking down. It does so at a steady rate. After about 5,600 years half the carbon-14 atoms have broken down; half are left.

After another 5,600 years, half of the half—a quarter—are left, and so on.

(Left) A Stone Age artist at Lascaux captured the energy of a horse in flight.

By measuring the amount of carbon 14 left, scientists can tell how long ago a plant or animal died. It's as if you set a kitchen timer for 40 minutes and someone says it will ring in 10 minutes—you then know it has been running for 30 minutes.

When the cave artists were at work, they often rubbed their torches on the cave wall to make them burn brighter. The rubbing left charcoal on the wall. Charcoal comes from wood, which came from a tree. By dating the charcoal, scientists may learn that the tree died, say, 25,000 years ago. This is about the same age as the charcoal—and gives them a date for when the painters were at work.

Carbon-14 dating is useful for dating material up to 40,000 years old. After that, almost no carbon 14 is left. For older material, scientists use other built-in blocks. One of these tells when hearth rocks were last heated or when flints fell into a fire and were heated.

Selected Bibliography

Bahn, Paul G., and Jean Vertut. *Images of the Ice Age*. New York: Facts on File, 1988.

Chauvet, Jean-Marie, Éliette Brunel Deschamps, and Christian Hillaire. *Dawn of Art: The Chauvet Cave*. New York: Harry N. Abrams, 1996.

Johanson, Donald, and Blake Edgar. *From Lucy to Language*. New York: Simon & Schuster, 1996.

Pfeiffer, John E. *The Creative Explosion: An Inquiry into the Origins of Art and Religion*. Ithaca, N.Y.: Cornell University Press, 1982.

Shreeve, James. *The Neandertal Enigma*. New York: William Morrow, 1995.

Tattersall, Ian. *The Last Neanderthal: The Rise, Success, and Mysterious Extinction of Our Closest Human Relatives*. New York: Macmillan, 1995.

Index

Illustration references are in **boldface.**

Africa: cave paintings 7
Animals: carvings **22–25;** cave paintings **6–11, 24–30, 34–45;** engravings 25–26, **32, 33;** migrations 17, 19
Antlers: shaman headdress **32;** tools **16,** 17
Ardèche River, France: gorges **4,** 5
Aurochs: cave paintings 6, **7, 28–30,** 31, **42–43**
Australia: cave paintings 7

Bears 29; carved head **25;** cave paintings 6, 34; fossils 6
Bison, European 29, 39; carved head **24;** cave paintings 6, **24–25,** 33, **40**
Bones, mammoth: houses and shelters 19, **19,** 20; used for fires 20
Bow and arrow: invention 17
Bulgaria: early modern humans 15

Calendar, bone **17**
Carbon-14 dating 45–46
Cattle, Ice Age *see* Aurochs
Cave paintings 5–6, **6–11,** 13, **24–31, 33–45;** artists 5, 9, 27, 29; map of sites **13;** meaning 31, 33–35; pigments 6, 26–27; scaffolds **28,** 29, 31; symbols 29, **36**
Chauvet, Jean-Marie 5–6, **6**
Chauvet Cave, near Avignon, France 5–7, 37, 39, 41; rock paintings **6–7, 38–41**
Cliffs, limestone: caves **4,** 5
Cro-Magnons *see* Humans, early modern

Dating methods *see* Carbon-14 dating

Engravings 25–26, 29, **32, 33;** tools 17, 25
Europe: arrival of early modern humans 9, 13, 15, 39; ice sheet 13; map of cave art sites **13**

Flint cores **14**
Flute, bird-bone **14–15**
Food preservation 19
Fossils 6, 9, 12, 15, 19, 21, 23

Hand stencils **1,** 6, **26, 27,** 29
Harpoon heads **16,** 17
Horses 6, 9, 29, 39; cave paintings **6, 8, 26–27, 30,** 31, **34–37, 44–45;** sculpture **22**
Humans, early modern 9, 12, 13, 15, 39; beliefs 31, 33–35; clothing 20, 23; fire 20, 21; food preparation **20–21;** hunting and fishing 15, **16–17,** 19, 36; inventions 15, **16–17, 20,** 36; jewelry 23, 25; lamps and torches 20, 28, 29, 34; musical instruments **14–15,** 15; physical characteristics 13; sewing 20, **20;** shamans **32,** 33–35; shelters and campsites 9, **18, 19,** 20, 21, 25; speech 21; tools and weapons **14–17,** 20, **24,** 25; trade 21

Ibex: drawing **16–17**
Ice Age 11, 12, 17, 35–36, 39; arrival of early modern humans 9, 13
Ivory carvings: animals **22–23,** 23; beads 23, human head **23**

Kilns: clay figures 20, 25
Lamps 20, **28–29**

Lascaux Cave, Montignac, France 39,
41; rock paintings **10–11, 24–25,
30–31, 34–35, 44–45**
Lions 6, 29; cave paintings 6, 31,
40–41; engraving **32**

Mammoths 19, 20, 22, 23, 29, 35; cave
paintings 6; engravings **33;** jaws **19**
Middle East: early people 9, 12, 15

Neanderthals 12, 15, 21; animal skin
clothing 20; computer image of
face **12;** fossils 12; hunting 15;
physical characteristics 13; shelters
19; tools and weapons **14–15,** 17;
use of fire 20
Needle, bone **20**

Panthers: cave paintings 39
Pech-Merle, France: cave painting
26–27; hand stencils **26, 27**
Plants 11, 15, 29, 36; cave painting
36–37; fossil pollen 21

Reindeer 11, 19, 31, 39; cave painting
10, drawing **16–17**
Rhinoceroses 29; cave paintings 6, **7,
8,** 31, **38–41**
Rivers: gorges **4,** 5; settlements 13
Rock-shelters 9, **18,** 19
Russia: prehistoric grave 23

Scrapers **14–15,** 17
Shamans **33–35;** antler headdress **32**
Spain: cave paintings 7; early modern
humans 15
Spear-throwers **16,** 17, **24**

Trois-Frères Cave, France: cave lion
engraving **32,** 33

Ukraine: food storage pits 19;
mammoth bone fires 20; Stone
Age house **19**

Illustration Credits

Alexander Marshack: p17, p22, p27; **Art Resource, NY:** p37; **CORBIS/Sygma:**
back cover (© Jean-Marie Chauvet/Le Seuil), p4 (© Maher Attar), p6
(© Jean-Marie Chauvet), p7 (© Jean-Marie Chauvet/Le Seuil), p8 (© Jean-Marie
Chauvet), p33 (© Jean-Marie Chauvet), p38 (© Jean-Marie Chauvet), p40–41
(two rhinos facing each other, © Jean-Marie Chauvet/Le Seuil);
David L. Brill: p14 (double-edged scraper tool, Institut du Quaternaire,
Batiment de Geologie, Universite de Bordeaux l), p14 (flint core tool, Denise de
Sonneville-Bordes, Centre Francois Bordes, Institut du Quaternaire, Batiment
de Geologie, Universite de Bordeaux l), p16 (antler harpoon head, R. Deffarge,
Institut du Quaternaire, Batiment de Geologie, Universite de Bordeaux l),
p16 (willow leaf point, Musee National de Prehistoire, Les Eyzies de Tayac),
p16 (end-scraper on a blade, Denise de Sonneville-Bordes, Centre Francois
Bordes, Institut du Quaternaire, Batiment de Geologie, Universite de Bordeaux
l), p20 (Societe Civile de Domaine de Pujol, Saint Girons), p24 (carved bison,
Musee des Antiquites Nationales, St. Germain-en-Laye), p25 (carved bear's
head, Musee des Antiquites Nationales, St. Germain-en-Laye); **De Sazo/
Photo Researchers:** front cover, p10; **Jean Vertut:** p24–25; **Lewis Sadler:** p12;
National Geographic Society: title page (© Sisse Brimberg), p15 (bird-bone
flute tool, Sisse Brimberg), p23 (human stone age, © Sisse Brimberg), p28
(fat-burning limestone, © Sisse Brimberg), p30 (© Sisse Brimberg), p34
(© Sisse Brimberg), p36 (© Sisse Brimberg), p40 (bison cave painting,
© Sisse Brimberg) p41 (cave lions, © Sisse Brimberg), p42 (chauvet,
© Sisse Brimberg), p44 (© Sisse Brimberg)